MW01703119

Specific Skill Series for Language Arts

Grammar

Leveled Books in Nine Key Language Arts Skill Areas

SRA

Columbus, OH

The McGraw-Hill Companies

Cover: ©PhotoDisc/Getty Images, Inc.

SRAonline.com

SRA

Send all inquiries to:
SRA/McGraw-Hill
8787 Orion Place
Columbus, OH 43240-4027

Printed in the United States of America.

ISBN 0-07-601701-X

3 4 5 6 7 8 9 RHR 14 13 12 11 10

TO THE TEACHER

GENERAL INFORMATION ON GRAMMAR

Grammar is the sound, structure, and meaning system of language. Traditional grammar study usually involves two areas: parts of speech and sentence structure or syntax. Parts of speech (nouns, verbs, adjectives, adverbs, pronouns, conjunctions) are typically considered to be the content of grammar. The parts of speech involve the *form* of English words. Sentence structure (subjects, predicates, objects, clauses, phrases) involves the *function* of the parts of speech.

The study of grammar is important for two reasons:

1. Educated people need to know and understand the structure of their language, which in large part defines their culture.
2. Knowledge of grammar gives teachers and students a common vocabulary for talking about language and makes discussions of writing tasks clearer and more efficient.

ABOUT *SPECIFIC SKILL SERIES FOR LANGUAGE ARTS*

Specific Skill Series for Language Arts is a companion to ***Specific Skill Series,*** a supplemental reading program that has been widely recognized for its effectiveness for over thirty years. The two series are designed and organized the same. ***Specific Skill Series for Language Arts*** consists of discrete units of practice exercises that target and reinforce fundamental language-arts skills. Units in both series are presented in multiple-choice format for standardized test practice.

ABOUT *GRAMMAR*

The scope and sequence for Books A through H of *Grammar* is based on traditional grammar study and focuses on parts of speech and sentence structure. The scope and sequence for each book is located on the last page of the book. Each unit includes

- **rule boxes** that explain grammar rules.
- **models** in each rule box to illustrate the language point being discussed.
- **multiple-choice exercises** for skills practice and reinforcement.

Four **Language Activity Pages** (LAPs) appear in each book. Each LAP is divided into the following four sections and reviews the skills practiced in the preceding units:

Exercising Your Skill reviews key terms and concepts.
Expanding Your Skill provides mixed practice.
Exploring Language shows how the skills apply to real-world contexts by featuring one of six forms of writing: descriptive, narrative, personal, persuasive, expository, and poetry.
Expressing Yourself includes two creative activities related to the skills. One activity is always a Work-with-a-Partner activity to encourage collaborative learning.

TO THE TEACHER

SERIES COMPONENTS

- **Student Editions:** Nine books in each level (A–H) focus on nine skill areas: *Grammar, Usage, Mechanics, Spelling, Vocabulary, Sentences, Paragraphs, Writing Process,* and *Research.*
- **Placement Test Books:** One book for each skill area includes diagnostic tests to place students in the correct level.
- **Teacher's Manual:** Primarily an answer key, the *Teacher's Manual* also includes reproducible student worksheets and further information on how to use the program, including classroom management tips.

HOW TO USE *SPECIFIC SKILL SERIES FOR LANGUAGE ARTS*

Placing Students in Levels: The scope and sequence, complexity of skills, and readability in Levels A through H correspond to Grades 1 through 8. Students may, however, be placed in any level. For example, in the second grade, a student who needs remedial work in a specific skill may be placed in Book A, an on-level student who would benefit from skills reinforcement may be placed in Book B, and an advanced student who is ready for enrichment may be placed in Book C or higher. *Placement Tests* help place students in the correct level.

Setting: This series can be used for independent study and one-on-one practice sessions, as well as in small-group and whole-class settings. It is also effective in after-school and summer-school programs.

Getting Started: Students must have notebook paper or copies of reproducible student worksheets (located in the *Teacher's Manual*) before they begin working. Remind students not to write in the books. Students may begin in any unit of any book, depending on the skill practice they need, although it is recommended that they begin with Unit 1. As they work through the units, students should record their answers on notebook paper or on the student worksheets.

Pacing: Students should be encouraged to work at their own pace, completing a few units every day or every other day.

Scoring: Teachers should score units as soon as they have been completed. Then a discussion can be held in which students justify their answer choices.

Internet Use: Some activities, especially those in *Research,* require students to use the Internet. Students' use of the Internet should be monitored closely for content appropriateness and safety.

TO THE STUDENT

Grammar refers to the basic parts of the English language and how to put these parts together to write sentences. Understanding grammar will help you communicate your ideas correctly and clearly when you speak and write.

In Book E *Grammar,* you will learn about

- Nouns
- Pronouns
- Verbs
- Adjectives
- Adverbs
- Prepositions
- Conjunctions
- Subjects and Predicates
- Direct and Indirect Objects
- Appositives
- Clauses
- Types of Sentences

After you complete this book, you will be able to label words and phrases based on how they function in a sentence.

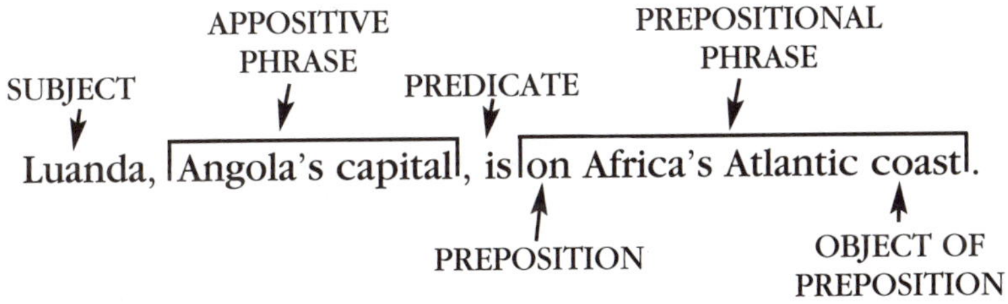

You will also learn about different types of clauses. In each sentence below, the boldfaced part is an example of the specified clause.

Independent Clause: **Portuguese is Angola's official language**.

Dependent Clause: Luanda is a port **because it is by the ocean**.

Adjective Clause: The government **that Angola upholds** is a republic.

Adverb Clause: **If you research Angola's economy**, you will find that sugarcane and bananas are two main crops.

By mastering the skills in this book, you will be able to use words correctly and effectively to communicate your ideas to other people.

Unit 1
Nouns

A **noun** is a word that names a person, a place, an animal, a thing, or an idea.

- A **common noun** names *any* person, place, animal, thing, or idea.
  man bird park statue hope
- A **proper noun** names a *particular* person, place, animal, thing, or idea. A proper noun begins with a capital letter.
  Mr. Richards Webber Park Statue of Liberty
- A **singular noun** names one: person, place, animal, thing, or idea. A **plural noun** names more than one; most plural nouns end in *-s* or *-es*, but some are irregular.

shoe—shoes	fox—foxes	wish—wishes	echo—echoes
county—counties	ox—oxen	woman—women	half—halves

New Orleans

Which of the underlined words in each sentence below is a noun?

1. The old (A) and beautiful (B) city of New Orleans is (C) in the state of Louisiana (D).

2. New Orleans (A) was founded (B) in 1719 and (C) originally belonged (D) to France.

3. In 1803 the city became (A) part of the United States when (B) land (C) was bought (D).

4. The (A) Louisiana Purchase doubled (B) the land belonging (C) to the United States (D).

5. New Orleans is (A) a busy (B) international port (C) located (D) on the Mississippi River.

6. Throughout (A) the year (B), New Orleans is (C) a popular (D) vacation destination.

7. Tourists (A) rarely (B) leave without trying (C) some (D) of Louisiana's Cajun cooking.

8. People return (A) to New Orleans to hear (B) great music (C) and eat tasty (D) food.

Unit 1

Nouns

The Farmers' Market

9. There are many products offered at the Riverton Farmers' Market.
(A) (B) (C) (D)

10. Families from all over the area come here to buy and sell.
(A) (B) (C) (D)

11. You can find fresh green beans, tomatoes, and squash at the market.
(A) (B) (C) (D)

12. The fruit stands have watermelon halves on sale for a good price.
(A) (B) (C) (D)

13. Some days there are even fresh fish, such as salmon or rainbow trout.
(A) (B) (C) (D)

14. A truck just arrived with many boxes of corn.
(A) (B) (C) (D)

15. Both of my brothers, who are farmers, sell produce here every week.
(A) (B) (C) (D)

16. You can buy other items at this market, including cheese and flowers.
(A) (B) (C) (D)

17. On the weekends, Mrs. Eugene sells crafts here that she makes at home.
(A) (B) (C) (D)

18. One of her best customers travels from West Virginia to buy her crafts.
(A) (B) (C) (D)

19. Coffee, tea, honey, herbs, and spices are also sold at the market.
(A) (B) (C) (D)

Unit 1

Nouns

A **compound noun** is a noun made of two or more words. If you know each word's meaning in a compound noun, sometimes you can decide what the compound noun means. For example, *houseguest* is a guest in a house.

- A **closed compound noun** is written as one word.
  bookmark teammate outdoors
- An **open compound noun** is written as more than one word.
  high school maid of honor living room
- The words in a **hyphenated compound noun** are joined by a hyphen (-). Check a dictionary if you are unsure of how to spell a compound noun.
  great-aunt father-in-law

Which underlined word or group of words in each sentence is a compound noun?

20. The runner-up (A) is a contestant (B) from Santa (C) Monica, California (D).

21. For her prizes (A), she won an Alaskan (B) cruise and chose (C) a houseboat (D).

22. My friend's (A) brother-in-law (B) is the contestant who (C) came in first place (D).

23. He (A) won a car, furniture (B) for his dining room (C), and a trip to Greece (D).

24. The game (A) they played (B) was a showcase (C) of facts and trivia (D).

25. Most people (A) mail (B) their game (C) entries at a local post office (D).

26. This way a time line (A) has been started (B) when they get (C) a receipt as proof (D).

27. Based on game (A) rules, postcards (B) are not accepted (C) as entries (D).

The Homestead

28. The land and the farmhouse have been in my family for many years.
(A) (B) (C) (D)

29. Our backyard has been a favorite spot for picnics, parties, and sports.
(A) (B) (C) (D)

30. We have played several ball games until it was too dark outside to see.
(A) (B) (C) (D)

31. A great-uncle I had never met came to one of our celebrations.
(A) (B) (C) (D)

32. He knew a lot about our family's history, and he was a great storyteller.
(A) (B) (C) (D)

33. Some stories were about homemade treats they made on weekends.
(A) (B) (C) (D)

34. My great-uncle and his family made ice cream in the summer months.
(A) (B) (C) (D)

35. Once summertime passed, they started to pick apples from their trees.
(A) (B) (C) (D)

36. They would use most of the apples to make delicious apple butter.
(A) (B) (C) (D)

37. In my family, get-togethers are special times for sharing food and stories.
(A) (B) (C) (D)

38. I hope my great-aunt will come to our next family gathering.
(A) (B) (C) (D)

Unit 2
Possessive Nouns

A **possessive noun** shows ownership, or possession, of things or qualities. It may be singular or plural.

- Singular possessive nouns are formed by adding an apostrophe (') and an *-s.*

  Carmen is studying at **Rosa's** house.

- Most plural nouns are formed by only adding an *-s.*

  The **boys'** shoes are in their lockers.

- Add an apostrophe and an *-s* to make most irregular plural nouns possessive. Irregular plural nouns do *not* end with *-s.*

  The **children's** bikes are in the driveway.

George Washington Carver

Is the underlined noun in each sentence written correctly?

1. George Washington Carver's birthplace was Diamond Grove, Missouri.
(A) Yes **(B)** No, change to Carvers'

2. In 1891, he became Iowa State Colleges' first African American student in Agriculture and Mechanic Arts.
(A) Yes **(B)** No, change to College's

3. In 1896, George Washington Carver completed a master's degree.
(A) Yes **(B)** No, change to masters'

4. He was then asked to teach at Alabama's Tuskegee Institute.
(A) Yes **(B)** No, change to Alabamas'

5. A large part of Carver's research uncovered the peanut's various uses.
(A) Yes **(B)** No, change to peanuts'

6. His work led to over 300 ways to improve peoples' lives with peanuts.
(A) Yes **(B)** No, change to people's

7. George Washington Carver died in 1943 and is remembered as one of the world's great teachers, scientists, and inventors.
(A) Yes **(B)** No, change to worlds'

Unit 2

Possessive Nouns

At the Museum

8. Carlos' class visited the Museum of Natural History.
(A) Yes **(B)** No, change to Carlos's

9. The guides' name was Mrs. Parson, and she knew a lot about the museum.
(A) Yes **(B)** No, change to guide's

10. Carlos was curious about a dinosaur's skeleton in the main hall.
(A) Yes **(B)** No, change to dinosaurs'

11. All the childrens' voices got really quiet when they saw it.
(A) Yes **(B)** No, change to children's

12. This animal's size was huge, and the animal could have been dangerous.
(A) Yes **(B)** No, change to animals'

13. Mrs. Parson told the children that this creature's diet was meat.
(A) Yes **(B)** No, change to creatures'

14. This meat eaters' noise must have frightened most other animals.
(A) Yes **(B)** No, change to meat eater's

15. The museum's theater was showing a movie about dinosaurs.
(A) Yes **(B)** No, change to museums'

16. The movie showed how dinosaurs' habitats may have looked.
(A) Yes **(B)** No, change to dinosaur's

17. After the movie, Mrs. Parson took us near the main halls' display again.
(A) Yes **(B)** No, change to hall's

18. She pointed to a fossil's mark and asked if we thought a dinosaur made it.
(A) Yes **(B)** No, change to fossils'

Unit 3

Subject and Object Pronouns

A **pronoun** is a word that can take the place of one or more nouns.

Alexis and I are cousins. ⟶ **We** are cousins.

- **Subject pronouns** are used in the subject part of a sentence. *I, you, he, she, it, we*, and *they* are subject pronouns.

  You like to skate. **They** skate a lot. **It** is a fun sport.

- **Object pronouns** are used as direct or indirect objects in the predicate part of a sentence. An object pronoun follows the main verb. *Me, you, him, her, it, us*, and *them* are object pronouns.

  Direct Object: I met **him** at school.

  Indirect Object: Can you give Noah and **me** money for lunch?

Coyotes

Choose the correct pronoun to complete each sentence.

1. Suki and _____ are writing a report together on coyotes.
   (A) me **(B)** I

2. _____ are wild dogs that live throughout regions of the United States.
   (A) They **(B)** Them

3. A park ranger helped Suki and _____ find information on coyotes.
   (A) me **(B)** I

4. _____ learned that less than 25% of coyote pups survive their first year.
   (A) Us **(B)** We

5. Coyotes are usually more afraid of humans than we are of _____.
   (A) they **(B)** them

6. The ranger told _____ that coyotes have different ways of howling.
   (A) us **(B)** we

7. With certain howls, _____ can express danger to other coyotes.
   (A) they **(B)** them

Unit 3
Subject and Object Pronouns

Plums

8. _____ read in a book that wild plums grew in the ancient city of Babylon.
(A) I **(B)** Me

9. At first, people used _____ for medicines, not for food.
(A) they **(B)** them

10. Europeans grew _____, and plums were also found in South America.
(A) they **(B)** them

11. _____ did not always taste the way they do today.
(A) They **(B)** Them

12. A friend told _____ that the book's author is a professor of agriculture.
(A) I **(B)** me

13. Some experts the author interviewed told _____ that European farmers tried to improve the bitter taste of their wild plums.
(A) he **(B)** him

14. _____ wrote how plums changed because of the efforts of the Europeans.
(A) He **(B)** Him

15. Over the years, _____ had produced plum trees with much sweeter fruit.
(A) they **(B)** them

16. _____ are familiar with sweet plums because America imported the trees.
(A) Us **(B)** We

17. In time, American plum trees provided _____ with a similarly sweet fruit.
(A) us **(B)** we

18. The book made _____ want to buy and plant my very own plum tree.
(A) I **(B)** me

Unit 3

Subject and Object Pronouns

Have You Ever Seen a Platypus?

In which sentence are pronouns used correctly?

19. **(A)** My brother and me went to the zoo.
    (B) Us saw an animal neither of we had ever seen before.
    (C) A zoo employee told us it was a platypus.
    (D) Me asked the handler, "What is a platypus?"

---

20. **(A)** Him said that these unique animals come from Australia.
    (B) Them live near lakes, rivers, and streams in burrows that they dig.
    (C) Them have a bill wider than a duck's, a body like an otter's, a tail like a beaver's, and webbed feet.
    (D) We were surprised to find out that the female platypus lays eggs.

---

21. **(A)** Typically, platypus eggs are just over half an inch long, and them are just under half an inch wide.
    (B) They are kept warm by the mother platypus.
    (C) Her protects the eggs, and the eggs hatch after ten to twelve days.
    (D) Platypus babies stay with the mother, and them get milk from she for three to four months.

---

22. **(A)** As them grow, platypuses eat prey including insects and mollusks.
    (B) Us asked the handler if platypuses have teeth.
    (C) Him said that adult platypuses do not have teeth.
    (D) He explained that they have grinding pads inside their mouths.

---

23. **(A)** My brother said him would like to learn more about platypuses.
    (B) Me agreed with my brother, so I asked the handler about male platypuses.
    (C) The handler said that they are larger than female platypuses.
    (D) However, both of they are smaller than house cats.

---

24. **(A)** We asked how male platypuses protect themselves.
    (B) Them have a poisonous spur on the inner side of each hind leg.
    (C) Then us asked, "Do platypuses make any noises?"
    (D) The handler told us that them are known to growl when threatened.

Unit 3

Subject and Object Pronouns

Our Grand Canyon Trip

25. **(A)** My family and me are going to the Grand Canyon National Park.
(B) Dad and Mom are buying bikes for I and my sister Lisa.
(C) They will bike with us on a path near the Rim Trail.
(D) Me and Lisa want to become junior park rangers.

26. **(A)** Dad read the park newspaper to us as soon as us arrived.
(B) Mom and him wanted to find the shuttle bus schedule.
(C) Lisa and I decided to go on a fossil walk later in the day.
(D) The booklet said us would see fossils of sea creatures!

27. **(A)** Mom bought us a book about animals that live in the park.
(B) She said her had seen a zebra-tailed lizard on one trail.
(C) Me and Lisa would like to see a canyon tree frog.
(D) Us were worried about seeing a Grand Canyon rattlesnake.

28. **(A)** A guide told we that humans have lived in the canyon for 4,000 years.
(B) Him said that many Native American tribes still live in the canyon.
(C) We asked him to show us figurines made by Native Americans.
(D) Them are made from twigs and are only a few inches tall.

29. **(A)** Mom and me were fascinated by the different layers of rock.
(B) We learned that the Grand Canyon was formed by erosion.
(C) Her and Lisa thought the red, green, and yellow walls were beautiful.
(D) Dad thought them were not as breathtaking as the Colorado River.

30. **(A)** In the park's forest, us saw many Ponderosa pine trees.
(B) Dad, Lisa, and me liked to look at the desert plants.
(C) Us discovered what them call a "pink rattlesnake" on the Tonto Trail.
(D) We thought the snake's skin was pretty.

Unit 4

Possessive Pronouns

A **possessive pronoun** shows ownership and may take the place of a possessive noun. Possessive pronouns do *not* use an apostrophe (').
They can be used before a noun or by themselves.

Here is **my** umbrella. Where is **yours**?

Possessive pronouns can be singular or plural.

Maya's umbrella is wet. ⟶ **Her** umbrella is wet.

Yong's and Kim's raincoats are soaked. ⟶ **Their** raincoats are soaked.

Possessive Pronouns Used Before Nouns
Singular: *my, your, his, her, its* Plural: *our, your, their*

Possessive Pronouns Used Alone
Singular: *mine, yours, his, hers, its* Plural: *ours, yours, theirs*

The Garden

Choose the possessive pronoun that correctly completes each sentence.

1. _____ brother and I planted a vegetable garden.
   (A) My **(B)** Mine

2. If you have never had a garden in _____ yard, you do not know how hard it is.
   (A) yours **(B)** your

3. The task of digging up the soil was _____.
   (A) mine **(B)** my

4. For planting, _____ choices were corn, peppers, squash, carrots, and beans.
   (A) ours **(B)** our

5. Our neighbors let us borrow _____ hose to water the garden regularly.
   (A) theirs **(B)** their

6. During the next several weeks, we weeded _____ garden.
   (A) our **(B)** ours

7. We liked sharing the vegetables, and our neighbors enjoyed _____.
   (A) their **(B)** theirs

Unit 4
Possessive Pronouns

Charleston

In which sentence are possessive pronouns used correctly?

8. **(A)** My sister and I visited mine Aunt Clara in Charleston, South Carolina.
   (B) This was ours first time in Charleston.
   (C) Our visit lasted for one week.

9. **(A)** We began ours visit by taking a carriage ride around the city.
   (B) The driver shared his knowledge of the city's history.
   (C) Aunt Clara grew up in Charleston, so she shared hers knowledge also.

10. **(A)** The next day we took our walking tour.
    (B) The beautiful gardens were ours favorite part of the tour.
    (C) Aunt Clara told us that some of theirs gardens were older than 100 years.

11. **(A)** My favorite part of the trip came later in the week.
    (B) We took a boat ride to Charleston's Fort Sumter on an island in it's harbor.
    (C) Mine sister told me that a Civil War battle took place at Fort Sumter.

12. **(A)** Hers favorite part of the trip was the Gibbes Art Museum.
    (B) As we walked around, my sister, aunt, and I saw it's beautiful artwork.
    (C) There were too many items to choose our favorite.

13. **(A)** On the day we planned ours picnic, it rained too hard to go.
    (B) Aunt Clara put a blanket of her on the covered porch for us to sit on.
    (C) Our porch picnic was the best ever!

14. **(A)** When the rain stopped, we each rented a bicycle of ours own.
    (B) My sister rode her bicycle the fastest out of the three of us.
    (C) Aunt Clara raced both of us on hers bicycle.

15. **(A)** After a wonderful week, it was time for our visit to end.
    (B) We thanked Aunt Clara for hers time and kindness.
    (C) She told us to visit hers house in Charleston anytime.

Unit 5
Pronouns

An **interrogative pronoun** asks a question. Use *who* to refer to people, and *whose* to show possession. Use *which* and *what* to refer to animals, things, and ideas.

Who was here? **Which** is yours? **What** happened?

A **demonstrative pronoun** points out something. A demonstrative pronoun may be singular or plural. *This* and *that* are singular. *These* and *those* are plural. *This* and *these* name something specific nearby. *That* and *those* name something specific at a distance.

This is a hat. **That** is a coat. **These** are shoes. **Those** are gloves.

River Discovery

Which type of pronoun is underlined in each sentence?

1. What is the longest river system in the United States?
   (A) interrogative **(B)** demonstrative

2. The answer to that is the Mississippi-Missouri river system.
   (A) interrogative **(B)** demonstrative

3. Who were the first Europeans to travel on the Mississippi River?
   (A) interrogative **(B)** demonstrative

4. Those were Spanish explorers, and they toured the river in the fourteenth century.
   (A) interrogative **(B)** demonstrative

5. These were not the only explorers because the French later settled in an area known as the Mississippi River Valley.
   (A) interrogative **(B)** demonstrative

6. Through which of the United States does the Mississippi-Missouri river system flow?
   (A) interrogative **(B)** demonstrative

7. These are some of the states where the river system flows: Arkansas, Illinois, Iowa, Louisiana, Mississippi, Missouri, Tennessee, and Wisconsin.
   (A) interrogative **(B)** demonstrative

Unit 5

Pronouns

A **reflexive pronoun** ends in *-self* or *-selves* and refers to the subject of a sentence.

Jamal watches **himself** practice sign language in the mirror.

An **intensive pronoun** ends in *-self* or *-selves* and draws attention to specific nouns or pronouns in a sentence.

Kendra and Isaac **themselves** found a good home for the puppy.

- Reflexive and intensive pronouns share the same singular and plural forms.

  Singular: *myself, yourself, himself, herself, itself*

  Plural: *ourselves, yourselves, themselves*

Lovely Landscapes

Which type of pronoun is underlined in each sentence?

8. I found myself browsing for flowers at the local garden center.
   (A) reflexive **(B)** intensive

9. My family themselves did most of our yard's landscaping.
   (A) reflexive **(B)** intensive

10. My mother bought herself a bench for the yard; she planned to sit on it and watch birds.
    (A) reflexive **(B)** intensive

11. My sister lined much of our yard with rocks herself.
    (A) reflexive **(B)** intensive

12. After she finished, she congratulated herself on a job well done.
    (A) reflexive **(B)** intensive

13. My father designed the layout of the trees himself.
    (A) reflexive **(B)** intensive

14. We all enjoy doing the landscaping ourselves.
    (A) reflexive **(B)** intensive

15. Even though planning can be difficult, the work itself is very satisfying.
    (A) reflexive **(B)** intensive

Unit 6
Pronouns

An **indefinite pronoun** is a pronoun that does *not* refer to a particular person, place, animal, or thing. Indefinite pronouns may be singular or plural.

- Singular indefinite pronouns include *anybody, anyone, anything, nobody, no one, nothing, each, one, either, everyone, everybody, someone, somebody*, and *something*.

  Everyone in my class wants to go on the field trip.

- Plural indefinite pronouns include *both, few, many, others*, and *several*.

  Many have already turned in their permission slips.

The Dog Show

Which of the underlined words is an indefinite pronoun?

1. It seemed as if everybody in town went to the dog show last week.
(A) It (B) everybody (C) went (D) show

2. You would have thought that there was nothing else going on in town.
(A) You (B) that (C) nothing (D) else

3. Someone helped the show's sponsors hang signs all over town.
(A) Someone (B) sponsors (C) signs (D) over

4. According to this show's rules, anybody with a dog could enter the show.
(A) According (B) anybody (C) could (D) show

5. A few entered uncommon dogs, such as Akitas and Samoyeds.
(A) few (B) uncommon (C) Akitas (D) Samoyeds

6. There were others who entered more common breeds.
(A) There (B) others (C) who (D) more

7. However, it turned out that the mutts were the favorites of everyone.
(A) it (B) that (C) favorites (D) everyone

Unit 6

Pronouns

If a singular indefinite pronoun is the subject of a sentence, use a singular pronoun to refer to it.

> **One** of the books does not have its cover.
>
> **Everyone** remembered his or her permission slip.

If a plural indefinite pronoun is the subject of a sentence, use a plural pronoun to refer to it.

> **Many** of the students brought their lunches from home.
>
> **Few** of us bought our lunches in the cafeteria.

Whippets

Are both of the underlined pronouns used correctly in each sentence?

8. Anyone who has a Whippet knows that their dog is a special breed.
   (A) Yes **(B)** No

9. Several of us think our Whippet is best described as a mini Greyhound.
   (A) Yes **(B)** No

10. Many of these animals were originally bred for their speed.
    (A) Yes **(B)** No

11. One of the Whippet's most distinctive features is their ability to race up to thirty-five miles per hour.
    (A) Yes **(B)** No

12. Both of my parents think of their Whippets as part of our family.
    (A) Yes **(B)** No

13. Each of the Whippets I have ever met has its own personality.
    (A) Yes **(B)** No

14. Nobody who decides to share their home with a Whippet will regret it.
    (A) Yes **(B)** No

The First LAP
Language Activity Pages

A. Exercising Your Skill

You have been learning about different types of nouns and pronouns. Number your paper from 1 to 10. Read the sentences below. Use a word from the box only once to complete each sentence correctly.

plural	reflexive	compound	possessive	object
indefinite	subject	interrogative	singular	pronoun

1. A _____ can take the place of one or more nouns.
2. _____ nouns or pronouns show ownership.
3. When a word is _____, it refers to one.
4. When a word is _____, it refers to more than one.
5. Examples of _____ pronouns are *anything, either*, and *none*.
6. An example of an _____ pronoun is *which*.
7. A _____ pronoun refers to the subject of a sentence.
8. A _____ noun combines two or more words.
9. In the predicate part of a sentence, _____ pronouns follow main verbs.
10. *I, you, he, she, it, we*, and *they* are _____ pronouns.

B. Expanding Your Skill

Number your paper from 1 to 8. Read the paragraph below. Use a pronoun from the box only once to complete each sentence correctly. Remember to capitalize any pronoun that is the first word of a sentence.

we	others	us	she
them	it	nobody	our

Most people from **(1)** _____ neighborhood attended last night's city council meeting. **(2)** _____ all signed a petition and presented it to the council. There were **(3)** _____ with letters from people who could not attend but felt the same way. **(4)** _____ at the meeting disagreed with the efforts to save Packer Park. There is a plan to destroy the park just to build another mall. Miss Rodriguez spoke to the members for all of **(5)** _____. **(6)** _____ suggested other sites for the new mall that already had empty buildings. The council listened carefully. They said that the people of the neighborhood had given **(7)** _____ a lot to consider. **(8)** _____ gave us hope that Packer Park might be saved.

C. Exploring Language

Persuasive Writing Number your paper from 1 to 16. Read the letter to the editor of a local newspaper below. Find nouns in the letter. Remember that there are many types of nouns. Some nouns might include two words, start with a capital letter, or show ownership. Write each noun on your paper.

To the editor:

I am against the city's plan to change Packer Park into a mall. I live near there on Spring Avenue. I sit in the park to enjoy the beautiful plants. My neighbors with children go there to play. There are already enough places to shop. More stores will mean more cars, and then more traffic and pollution. Worse yet, we will lose a natural space we all can enjoy.

D. Expressing Yourself

Choose one of these activities. When you are finished, give your paper to your teacher.

1. Write your own brief letter to the editor of a local newspaper. Write about a change you would like to see happen where you live. Correctly use some of the different types of nouns and pronouns you have learned. For example, *Many people in my neighborhood share this opinion. People, neighborhood,* and *opinion* are nouns, and *my* is a possessive pronoun. Be sure to include possible solutions if you write about a problem. You may also write about ideas for your community that do not solve a problem, such as suggesting an event or a celebration for your town.

2. **WORK with a PARTNER** Find a partner, and choose an article from a newspaper or a magazine. Together, search for all the nouns in the article. Underline the nouns, or write them on a sheet of paper. Remember to include proper and possessive nouns in your search. Now take turns replacing as many of the nouns as you can with their correct pronouns. Write both the noun and its pronoun on your paper. Take time to check each other's work. Be sure to attach the article to your paper when you turn in your work.

Unit 7
Verbs

A **verb** is a word that shows action or expresses a state of being.

- An **action verb** shows what the subject of the sentence does or has.

  Darcel **rides** her bike around the block.
- A **linking verb** expresses a state of being or a condition and links the subject in a sentence to a noun, a pronoun, or an adjective in the predicate. Common linking verbs include *am, is, are, was, were, be, being*, and *been*.

  I **am** a student. Jerome **is** a teacher.
- These words can function as either an action verb or a linking verb: *look, taste, smell, feel, sound, grow, stay, appear*, and *remain*.

  Action: Lois **tastes** the pear. Linking: The pear **tastes** good.

Freshwater Habitats

Which type of verb is the underlined word in each sentence?

1. Living things in freshwater <u>are</u> different from those on land or in the sea.
   (A) action verb **(B)** linking verb

2. Flowering plants <u>grow</u> near the edge of the water.
   (A) action verb **(B)** linking verb

3. Some plants <u>float</u> in lakes and ponds.
   (A) action verb **(B)** linking verb

4. Many freshwater animals <u>live</u> only part of their lives in water.
   (A) action verb **(B)** linking verb

5. For example, a frog <u>is</u> in the water in the early stage of its life.
   (A) action verb **(B)** linking verb

6. Frogs <u>become</u> land animals as they grow, but adult frogs stay close to water.
   (A) action verb **(B)** linking verb

7. The otter <u>makes</u> its home on land but gathers food underwater.
   (A) action verb **(B)** linking verb

8. A variety of birds <u>divide</u> their time between water and land.
   (A) action verb **(B)** linking verb

Unit 7
Verbs

In some sentences, the verb is one word. In other sentences, the verb is made of two or more words. In these cases the last verb is the **main verb.** The other verbs are the **helping verbs.** They help the main verb express action or make a statement.

Ethan and Roberto **will ride** the bus home.

HELPING VERB ↑ will — MAIN VERB ↑ ride

Common helping verbs are *do, did, does, am, is, are, was, were, be, being, been, have, has, had, may, might, must, can, could, will, would, shall*, and *should*.

- When a verb includes more than one word, it is a **verb phrase.** A phrase is a group of words, and a verb phrase is a group of words that acts as a verb.

  They **may have been waiting** for you.

The Star-Spangled Banner

Is the underlined word or group of words in each sentence a main verb, a helping verb, or a verb phrase?

9. "The Star-Spangled Banner" became America's unofficial national anthem nearly forty years after winning its independence from England.
(A) main verb **(B)** helping verb **(C)** verb phrase

10. Therefore, it seems odd that the song's melody is British.
(A) main verb **(B)** helping verb **(C)** verb phrase

11. The song's words were written by Francis Scott Key.
(A) main verb **(B)** helping verb **(C)** verb phrase

12. Colonists had been singing different words to the melody for years.
(A) main verb **(B)** helping verb **(C)** verb phrase

13. The song gained popularity and was adopted as the national anthem in 1931.
(A) main verb **(B)** helping verb **(C)** verb phrase

14. Today the flag that inspired Francis Scott Key can be found in the Smithsonian Institution in Washington, D.C.
(A) main verb **(B)** helping verb **(C)** verb phrase

Unit 8

Adjectives

An **adjective** is a word that modifies, or describes, a noun or a pronoun and answers the question *how many, what kind*, or *which one*. An adjective can come before or after the word it describes.

seven sisters **blue** shirt **that** window It is **small**.

- A **proper adjective** is formed from a proper noun. It begins with a capital letter.

  American citizen **English** muffin **Mexican** festival

- Certain verb forms can also be adjectives. They are called **participles.**

  Present participle: The **sleeping** girl is my sister.

  Past participle: The **broken** racquet belongs to Keesha.

Snakes

Is the underlined word in each sentence an adjective?

1. Snakes are remarkable reptiles without legs or external ears.
   (A) Yes **(B)** No

2. Some venomous snakes inject prey with venom using hollow fangs.
   (A) Yes **(B)** No

3. A Florida snake called the timber rattlesnake is one example of a venomous snake.
   (A) Yes **(B)** No

4. Constricting snakes can squeeze their prey to death.
   (A) Yes **(B)** No

5. Snakes live on the ground, under the ground, in trees, and in water.
   (A) Yes **(B)** No

6. Some snakes can shed their skin up to six times per year.
   (A) Yes **(B)** No

7. On record, the shortest snake is just over four inches in length, and the longest is over thirty feet in length.
   (A) Yes **(B)** No

Unit 8
Adjectives

- A **compound adjective** is made by combining two or more words. The words are joined with a hyphen (-) when the compound adjective comes before the noun or pronoun it describes.

  some **fresh-baked** bread a **six-year-old** car

- A **demonstrative adjective** describes a noun by answering the question *which one* or *which ones*. The words *this, that, these*, and *those* can be used as demonstrative adjectives. They point out something specific.

  This backpack belongs to me. **These** rolls are warm.

Winged Predators

Which of the underlined words is an adjective?

8. Most birds (A) of prey (B) have huge wings, hooked (C) beaks, and sharp claws (D).

9. These (A) birds are (B) powerful and (C) efficient hunters (D).

10. They (A) have well-developed (B) wings and very (C) sharp vision (D).

11. Their eyesight (A) may be as much (B) as eight (C) times better than (D) that of humans.

12. The golden (A) eagle (B) is one of the largest and most (C) powerful birds of prey (D).

13. When (A) a brand-new (B) eagle chick hatches, he or she has fluffy, white feathers that (C) feel very soft and look (D) very different from adult golden eagles.

14. Once fully grown, some of these (A) birds can carry (B) prey weighing (C) up to ten pounds (D).

15. An adult golden eagle's (A) impressive wingspan (B) can be over (C) seven (D) feet.

Unit 9
Adverbs

An **adverb** is a word that modifies, or describes, a verb, an adjective, or another adverb. Each underlined word in the examples below is the word the adverb describes. Adverbs answer these questions:

How: Ben **proudly** showed me shells he found.

When: **Then** we ate lunch on the beach.

Where: We got **there** around noon.

To what degree: The beach was **very** lovely.

Endangered Animals

Is the underlined word in each sentence an adverb?

1. There are many seriously endangered animals in the world.
   (A) Yes **(B)** No

2. Some species are disappearing at a very alarming rate.
   (A) Yes **(B)** No

3. Human beings are partly responsible for this situation.
   (A) Yes **(B)** No

4. Scientists now say that thousands of species may become extinct within twenty years.
   (A) Yes **(B)** No

5. Elephants are hunted for their ivory tusks.
   (A) Yes **(B)** No

6. Tigers are hunted for their beautifully striped coats.
   (A) Yes **(B)** No

7. Many dolphins become helpless victims trapped in ordinary fishing nets.
   (A) Yes **(B)** No

8. It is important not to wait until a later date to protect endangered animals.
   (A) Yes **(B)** No

Unit 9
Adverbs

Many adverbs often have *-ly* endings, but some do not.

carefully smoothly quietly

In the sentence *She **gently** closed the door*, the adverb *gently* tells how the door was closed.

- There are a few *-ly* words that are not adverbs. The *-ly* words below are adjectives because they describe nouns and pronouns.

  lonely lively friendly lovely kindly

In the sentence *The **friendly** dog wags her tail*, the adjective *friendly* describes the dog and not the dog's action (*wags*).

Endangered Plants

Which of the underlined words is an adverb?

9. Nearly (A) twenty-five percent (B) of the world's (C) plants are in danger (D) of extinction.

10. This (A) situation is mainly (B) due to the destruction (C) of plants' habitats (D).

11. Plants (A) that grow (B) on islands (C) are particularly (D) vulnerable.

12. Island (A) plants can (B) be more easily (C) destroyed by climate (D) changes.

13. Plants that are burned (A) and cleared (B) for farming (C) are rapidly (D) disappearing in rain forests.

14. Many (A) species (B) of plants that grow there (C) will be (D) lost forever.

15. The loss (A) of rain forests is extremely (B) serious because (C) of oxygen they supply (D).

Unit 10

Prepositions

A **preposition** relates a noun or a pronoun to another word in a sentence. It often expresses time or place. Common prepositions include *about, above, across, after, against, along, among, around, at, before, behind, below, beneath, between, by, down, during, for, from, in, near, of, off, on, out, over, through, to, under, up,* and *with.*

We will leave **after** breakfast. We are **near** the post office.

- The noun or pronoun that follows a preposition is called the **object of the preposition.**

  We should be home **by noon**.

  ↑ PREPOSITION ↑ OBJECT OF PREPOSITION

- A **prepositional phrase** is a group of words that begins with a preposition and ends with the object of the preposition, which is a noun or a pronoun.

  We drove **over a rickety old bridge**.

Hot Deserts

Are only prepositional phrases underlined in each sentence?

1. In some parts of the world, the temperature is extremely hot.
   (A) Yes **(B)** No

2. The lack of water makes a hot desert a difficult place to live.
   (A) Yes **(B)** No

3. Some desert plants have very tough leaves and roots.
   (A) Yes **(B)** No

4. Other plants have seeds that wait in the ground for years to sprout.
   (A) Yes **(B)** No

5. Desert animals have also adapted to life in the extreme heat.
   (A) Yes **(B)** No

6. Fennec Foxes stay in burrows during the day and come out for cooler nights.
   (A) Yes **(B)** No

7. In addition, this fox is able to lose extra body heat through its large ears.
   (A) Yes **(B)** No

Unit 10

Prepositions

Life in a Polar Region

8. Most of the Arctic is a huge sheet of ice that floats on the Arctic Ocean.
(A) Yes (B) No

9. The land surrounding the Arctic Ocean is known as the tundra.
(A) Yes (B) No

10. In this icy polar region it is difficult for land animals to travel or find food.
(A) Yes (B) No

11. Some animals that live there develop a thick coat or a special blood type.
(A) Yes (B) No

12. Other animals develop a thick layer of fat under their coat or skin.
(A) Yes (B) No

13. Still others have a dense layer of feathers to cover their stored fat.
(A) Yes (B) No

14. The most successful plants in the Arctic are mosses, lichen, and algae.
(A) Yes (B) No

15. Much plant life of the Arctic can survive the force of sweeping winds.
(A) Yes (B) No

16. The soil that is frozen permanently in the tundra is called permafrost.
(A) Yes (B) No

17. The Arctic's growing season is a brief cycle.
(A) Yes (B) No

18. Though the climate is harsh, insects hatch during the short summers.
(A) Yes (B) No

Unit 11
Conjunctions

A **conjunction** is a word that connects words or groups of words.

- A **coordinating conjunction** connects compound parts of a sentence. The words *and, but*, and *or* are coordinating conjunctions.

  Dogs **and** cats have whiskers. (connects two subjects)

  Cats can live in a house **or** in an apartment. (connects two objects)

  Many people like cats, **but** I prefer dogs. (connects main clauses)

- **Correlative conjunctions** work in pairs to connect compound parts of a sentence. *Either-or* and *neither-nor* are correlative conjunctions.

  Either Regina **or** I will feed the animals.

  Neither Marcus **nor** Kara will be able to help.

The Deep Ocean

Which type of conjunction is underlined in each sentence?

1. Many strange-looking creatures swim or crawl around in an ocean.
   (A) coordinating **(B)** correlative

2. The deepest part of an ocean is very dark and mysterious.
   (A) coordinating **(B)** correlative

3. Neither light nor heat from the sun reaches an ocean's depths.
   (A) coordinating **(B)** correlative

4. Most of the deep ocean is extremely cold, but there are places where hot water gushes through cracks in the ocean floor.
   (A) coordinating **(B)** correlative

5. Creatures such as giant tube worms and blind white crabs live around these cracks.
   (A) coordinating **(B)** correlative

6. These animals depend on neither sunlight nor plants for food.
   (A) coordinating **(B)** correlative

7. The deep ocean may seem unfit for living things, but it is full of them.
   (A) coordinating **(B)** correlative

Unit 11
Conjunctions

A **subordinating conjunction** introduces a subordinate, or dependent, clause. A dependent clause has a subject and a verb, but it cannot stand alone as a sentence because it does not express a complete thought. Common subordinating conjunctions include *after, although, as, because, before, if, since, than, unless, until, when, whenever, where, wherever*, and *while*.

Please finish your work **before** you leave.

Caving

What type of conjunction is underlined in each sentence?

8. It is important to be prepared when you explore caves.
   (A) coordinating **(B)** correlative **(C)** subordinating

9. Boots with strong support and good tread are essential.
   (A) coordinating **(B)** correlative **(C)** subordinating

10. Knee and elbow pads protect against scrapes and bruises as you explore.
    (A) coordinating **(B)** correlative **(C)** subordinating

11. Either a caving hat or a construction hardhat is required for safety.
    (A) coordinating **(B)** correlative **(C)** subordinating

12. Cavers take a head lantern, a flashlight, and matches while they cave.
    (A) coordinating **(B)** correlative **(C)** subordinating

13. Cavers should wear jeans and long-sleeved shirts because they reduce cuts.
    (A) coordinating **(B)** correlative **(C)** subordinating

14. One great pleasure of caving is finding unknown or unexplored caves.
    (A) coordinating **(B)** correlative **(C)** subordinating

15. Neither an expert nor an amateur should go caving alone.
    (A) coordinating **(B)** correlative **(C)** subordinating

A. Exercising Your Skill

You have been learning about different types of verbs, adjectives, adverbs, prepositions, and conjunctions. Number your paper from 1 to 10. Read the sentences below. Use a word from the box only once to complete each sentence correctly.

proper	subordinating	adverb	conjunction	adjective
correlative	preposition	demonstrative	coordinating	helping

1. An _____ modifies or describes a noun or a pronoun.
2. An _____ modifies or describes a verb, an adjective, or an adverb.
3. A _____ adjective begins with a capital letter.
4. A _____ adjective answers the question *which one* or *which ones*?
5. A _____ verb comes before the main verb in a sentence.
6. A _____ often expresses time or place in a sentence.
7. A _____ connects words or groups of words.
8. A _____ conjunction introduces a dependent clause.
9. _____ conjunctions work in pairs to join compound parts of a sentence.
10. A _____ conjunction is one word that connects compound parts of a sentence.

B. Expanding Your Skill

Number your paper from 1 to 10. Read the newspaper article below. Each underlined word is a preposition or a conjunction. On your paper, write **prep** if the underlined word is a preposition. Write **conj** if the underlined word is a conjunction.

Local Food Store Grand Opening

The opening <u>of</u> the Jumbo Save Food Store <u>on</u> Friday at the Rockingham Mall was a hit! The manager <u>and</u> the employees were happy <u>about</u> the number of customers. <u>When</u> she was asked, the manager said that the opening was a success. Customers were pleased <u>with</u> special sales. In fact, many customers lined up <u>at</u> the store's door <u>before</u> it opened. They were excited about the half-price offer on produce <u>or</u> dairy. Sales were good, <u>but</u> the manager expects better figures in future weeks.

C. Exploring Language

Expository Writing Number your paper from 1 to 10. Read the paragraph below. Each underlined word is a verb, an adjective, or an adverb. Write the letter **V** on your paper if the word is a verb. Write **ADJ** on your paper if the word is an adjective. Write **ADV** on your paper if the word is an adverb.

Tennessee is known as "The Volunteer State." It got the nickname because of soldiers in the War of 1812 who bravely volunteered to fight for freedom. Nashville is the charming capital of the state. It is home to the largest popular music museum in the world. Another main city in Tennessee is Knoxville. Knoxville has three national parks surrounding it. One of these parks is the Great Smoky Mountains National Park. This park extends into North Carolina also. Beautiful views of the mountains are easily found in Knoxville.

D. Expressing Yourself

Choose one of these activities. When you are finished, give your paper to your teacher.

1. Imagine that you are a photographer. Write three sentences to tell how you plan to take pictures to go with a newspaper article about a new library that is opening. In your sentences, be sure to include some of the different parts of speech you have learned. For example, *I would get there before the library closed so people would be in my photograph.* The word *closed* is a verb, and *would get* and *would be* are verb phrases. The word *there* is an adverb, the word *before* is a subordinating conjunction, and *in my photograph* is a prepositional phrase.

2. **WORK with a PARTNER** Work with a partner to find a photograph in a newspaper or a magazine. The photograph you choose should have a caption, or a short description. Save the caption, but set it aside during this activity. With your partner, write a new caption for the photograph. Be sure to accurately describe what is in the photograph using several parts of speech you have learned. For example, *That skunk proudly struts down the street. That* is a demonstrative adjective, *proudly* is an adverb, *struts* is a verb, and *down the street* is a prepositional phrase. If there is time, compare your caption to the original. Include the original caption with yours to give to your teacher.

Unit 12
Subjects and Predicates

A **sentence** has two main parts: a **subject** and a **predicate.** The subject part of a sentence tells whom or what the sentence is about.

Joe ran a marathon.

- The **simple subject** is the main word or word group that does something or is described.

  The **marathon** was in Cleveland.

- A **compound subject** is two or more simple subjects that share the same predicate and are joined by *and, or, either. . .or,* or *neither. . .nor.* A compound subject shares the same verb.

  Runners and walkers followed different marathon routes.

Mountain Lions

Is the subject in each sentence simple or compound?

1. Various areas and habitats are home to the mountain lion.
   (A) simple **(B)** compound

2. This widely distributed cat is also known as the *cougar, panther*, or *puma*.
   (A) simple **(B)** compound

3. These territorial hunters are not like most cat species.
   (A) simple **(B)** compound

4. They may be active during the day.
   (A) simple **(B)** compound

5. The behavior or action of a mountain lion is similar to that of house cats.
   (A) simple **(B)** compound

6. Sometimes house cats can be seen sneaking up on birds, mice, or even bugs.
   (A) simple **(B)** compound

7. Pounces or attacks are a mountain lion's strategies for surprising its prey.
   (A) simple **(B)** compound

8. Campers and hikers would be wise to avoid this and other wild animals.
   (A) simple **(B)** compound

Unit 12
Subjects and Predicates

A sentence's **complete subject** includes the simple subject plus any words that modify or describe it. In this example, the simple subject is underlined.

The marathon in Cleveland was last Saturday.

Dinosaurs

Is the underlined subject in each sentence complete?

9. Some of the most dangerous dinosaurs were birdlike predators.
   (A) Yes **(B)** No

10. Some of these carnivores were small and fast.
    (A) Yes **(B)** No

11. Their long, sharp teeth were deadly.
    (A) Yes **(B)** No

12. Winglike arms gave them balance during a chase.
    (A) Yes **(B)** No

13. A claw on the middle toe of each foot was used for slashing.
    (A) Yes **(B)** No

14. They may have hunted in packs.
    (A) Yes **(B)** No

15. Many large animals could be attacked in this way.
    (A) Yes **(B)** No

16. Dinosaurs that lived long ago may have animal relatives that live today.
    (A) Yes **(B)** No

17. Most birds are thought to be relatives of meat-eating dinosaurs.
    (A) Yes **(B)** No

18. Several reptiles may be related to animals that lived before dinosaurs.
    (A) Yes **(B)** No

Unit 12
Subjects and Predicates

The predicate part of a sentence tells what the subject does, has, is, or is like. The predicate usually comes after the subject.

Anitra **sketched** a self-portrait.

- The **simple predicate** is the main word or word group that tells what the subject does, has, is, or is like.

  She **decided** to frame it.

- A **compound predicate** is two or more simple predicates, or verbs that share the same subject and are joined by *and, or, but, either. . .or,* or *neither. . .nor*. A compound predicate shares the same subject.

  Anitra **painted and cut** the portrait.

Starfish

Is the predicate in each sentence simple or compound?

19. Starfish are among the world's most unusual creatures.
(A) simple (B) compound

20. These odd animals move and travel in any direction without turning.
(A) simple (B) compound

21. Unlike most animals, they lack a front and a back.
(A) simple (B) compound

22. Most starfish have five or six limbs.
(A) simple (B) compound

23. They squeeze or wedge into cracks of rocks by rearranging their limbs.
(A) simple (B) compound

24. In the water starfish feel mushy to touch.
(A) simple (B) compound

25. They become very stiff out of water.
(A) simple (B) compound

26. Some starfish stiffen or harden when you try to hold them.
(A) simple (B) compound

Unit 12

Subjects and Predicates

A sentence's **complete predicate** includes the simple predicate plus any words that describe it or add to its meaning. In this example, the simple predicate is underlined.

Anitra **gave the portrait to her parents for their anniversary**.

Animal Communication

Are the underlined words in each sentence a complete predicate?

27. Animals communicate and understand each other in different ways.
(A) Yes (B) No

28. Some spiders send signals to each other by plucking strands of their webs.
(A) Yes (B) No

29. Monkeys call out to warn other members of their group about predators.
(A) Yes (B) No

30. A mother fur seal seeks and finds her pups by barking.
(A) Yes (B) No

31. A kangaroo thumps its back legs to warn other kangaroos of danger.
(A) Yes (B) No

32. Whales and dolphins can produce complex underwater sounds.
(A) Yes (B) No

33. An elephant uses its trunk to show care and affection.
(A) Yes (B) No

34. Giraffes press their necks together when they like one another.
(A) Yes (B) No

35. Many animals do a special dance to get the attention of the same species.
(A) Yes (B) No

36. We may never know what some animal communication means.
(A) Yes (B) No

Unit 13

Direct and Indirect Objects

A **direct object** is a noun or a pronoun that receives the action of a verb. It answers the question *what* or *whom*. A direct object always comes after an action verb.

Answers *what*: Louise washed **cars** today.

Answers *whom*: Enrique drove **Peter** home.

However, not all action verbs are followed by direct objects. A sentence does *not* have a direct object if there is not a word that follows an action verb and answers *what* or *whom*.

No Direct Object: They smiled in the photograph.

Honeybees

Is the underlined word in each sentence a direct object?

1. Bees have ways of communicating that are very effective.
   (A) Yes **(B)** No

2. For example, a bee can tell others where to find nectar-rich flowers.
   (A) Yes **(B)** No

3. The bee dances in a way that depends on what it wants to communicate.
   (A) Yes **(B)** No

4. One type of dance shows how close the flowers are to the hive.
   (A) Yes **(B)** No

5. Another dance gives locations of exactly where to find the flowers.
   (A) Yes **(B)** No

6. This communication works for the bees.
   (A) Yes **(B)** No

7. It makes bees efficient gatherers of nectar.
   (A) Yes **(B)** No

8. Bees have to visit nearly two million flowers to make one pound of honey.
   (A) Yes **(B)** No

Unit 13
Direct and Indirect Objects

Pineapples

Which of the underlined words is a direct object?

9. We tasted pineapples that were ripe and fresh from the field.
(A) We **(B)** tasted **(C)** pineapples **(D)** fresh

10. My sister Antonia asked questions about how to grow pineapples.
(A) sister **(B)** Antonia **(C)** questions **(D)** how

11. My mom snapped photos of us with one of the pineapple farmers.
(A) mom **(B)** photos **(C)** one **(D)** farmers

12. Originally, people of South America grew pineapples.
(A) Originally **(B)** people **(C)** grew **(D)** pineapples

13. Various explorers transported plants to grow pineapples in Europe.
(A) explorers **(B)** transported **(C)** plants **(D)** Europe

14. Europeans introduced pineapples to Australia and Hawaii late in the 1700s.
(A) Europeans **(B)** pineapples **(C)** Australia **(D)** Hawaii

15. Today the country of China produces pineapples as well.
(A) Today **(B)** country **(C)** China **(D)** pineapples

16. We sent postcards of a pineapple plantation to some friends back home.
(A) postcards **(B)** pineapple **(C)** plantation **(D)** friends

17. My dad mailed recipes to many family members.
(A) dad **(B)** recipes **(C)** family **(D)** members

18. The recipes show pineapples used in salads, desserts, and main courses.
(A) recipes **(B)** show **(C)** pineapples **(D)** desserts

19. I prepared bread with pineapple and pecans after reading some recipes.
(A) bread **(B)** pineapple **(C)** pecans **(D)** reading

Unit 13

Direct and Indirect Objects

An **indirect object** is a noun or a pronoun that answers the question *to whom, for whom, to what*, or *for what* an action is done. Indirect objects are only in sentences with direct objects. They occur between the verb and the direct object.

Answers *to whom:* Dawn gave **me** the scrapbook.

Answers *for whom:* Ray bought his **cousin** a present.

Answers *to what:* Monica gave her **dog** a toy.

Answers *for what:* Eddie bought our **car** wax.

No Indirect Object: I called you after the game.

Sharks

Is the underlined word in each sentence an indirect object?

20. My grandparents bought <u>us</u> tickets to the aquarium.
(A) Yes (B) No

21. I watched <u>sharks</u> most of the time.
(A) Yes (B) No

22. My grandma told <u>me</u> some facts about sharks.
(A) Yes (B) No

23. Most <u>sharks</u> lose their teeth frequently.
(A) Yes (B) No

24. It takes <u>them</u> no time at all to replace their teeth.
(A) Yes (B) No

25. Sharks have new <u>ones</u> that push forward to where the old teeth were.
(A) Yes (B) No

26. Some sharks replace 30,000 teeth in a <u>lifetime</u>.
(A) Yes (B) No

27. My grandpa gave <u>me</u> a souvenir from the aquarium.
(A) Yes (B) No

Unit 13
Direct and Indirect Objects

Ostriches

Is the underlined object in each sentence direct or indirect?

28. Ostriches, the largest living birds, mainly eat <u>plants</u>.
(A) direct object **(B)** indirect object

29. Conservation gives an <u>ostrich</u> the chance to live for days without water.
(A) direct object **(B)** indirect object

30. Ostriches can give <u>people and animals</u> a forceful kick if threatened.
(A) direct object **(B)** indirect object

31. To avoid being seen, they may extend their <u>necks</u> while on the ground.
(A) direct object **(B)** indirect object

32. This gives <u>others</u> the wrong idea that ostriches bury their heads in the ground.
(A) direct object **(B)** indirect object

33. Ostriches use their <u>speed</u> to escape, as they are the fastest two-legged animal.
(A) direct object **(B)** indirect object

34. Males have brighter <u>hues</u>, usually black and white, and can be nine feet tall.
(A) direct object **(B)** indirect object

35. Grayish-brown colors give the shorter female <u>ostriches</u> a plain look.
(A) direct object **(B)** indirect object

36. An ostrich nest, which is a hole in the ground, holds fifteen to sixty <u>eggs</u>.
(A) direct object **(B)** indirect object

37. Females and males give <u>eggs</u> attention before they hatch in about forty days.
(A) direct object **(B)** indirect object

38. A female can recognize her own <u>eggs</u> even in a communal nest.
(A) direct object **(B)** indirect object

Unit 14
Appositives

An **appositive** is a noun used to identify or give more information about another noun. An appositive is always next to the noun it modifies. When it is *not* essential to a sentence, an appositive is set off with commas. In the example below, Robert had only one father, so *Abraham* is not essential.

Robert Todd Lincoln's father, **Abraham**, was born in 1809.

If an appositive is essential to a sentence's meaning, commas are *not* used. In the example below, *Joyce* is not set off with commas because Glenn has more than one neighbor. *Joyce* is essential to the sentence so the reader knows which of Glenn's neighbors is referred to.

Glenn's neighbor **Joyce** likes to read about past presidents.

The Planetarium

Is the underlined part of each sentence an appositive?

1. Our science teacher, <u>Miss Rydell</u>, took us to the planetarium.
   (A) Yes **(B)** No

2. A planetarium is <u>a place</u> with powerful telescopes to view outer space.
   (A) Yes **(B)** No

3. My brother <u>Jack</u> knows a lot about these huge telescopes.
   (A) Yes **(B)** No

4. He took <u>a course</u> offered by the planetarium.
   (A) Yes **(B)** No

5. Our <u>class</u> got to see a film in the planetarium's theater.
   (A) Yes **(B)** No

6. My classmate <u>Cyrus</u> thought the film was the best part of our field trip.
   (A) Yes **(B)** No

7. I enjoyed <u>our chance</u> to identify constellations in a specially lit room.
   (A) Yes **(B)** No

8. Mr. Cortez, <u>our guide</u>, led us to the largest telescope at the end of the day.
   (A) Yes **(B)** No

Unit 14
Appositives

The Storm

9. The battered ship, *Proud Glory*, crashed again and again against the waves.
(A) Yes **(B)** No

---

10. Passengers said it was nearly impossible to hear over the howling wind.
(A) Yes **(B)** No

---

11. The ship's captain, Lance Polk, ordered his crew to prepare the lifeboats.
(A) Yes **(B)** No

---

12. My friend Samantha Geller was a member of the ship's crew.
(A) Yes **(B)** No

---

13. Samantha survived the wreck, but the ship did not.
(A) Yes **(B)** No

---

14. Her supervisor, Joel Franklin, had experience with ships and storms.
(A) Yes **(B)** No

---

15. Everybody aboard the ship piled into the lifeboats with time to spare.
(A) Yes **(B)** No

---

16. The lights of the rescue boat, *Anchors Away*, were a welcome sight.
(A) Yes **(B)** No

---

17. Suddenly all crew members, passengers, and rescuers were silent.
(A) Yes **(B)** No

---

18. With a mighty splash, the hopeless ship split apart and sank beneath the waves.
(A) Yes **(B)** No

---

19. Survivor Otis Coleman said he would not be afraid to sail again.
(A) Yes **(B)** No

Unit 14
Appositives

An **appositive phrase** is a group of words that includes an appositive and other words that modify the appositive. An appositive phrase identifies or adds information to a noun and appears next to that noun.

Abraham Lincoln, **our sixteenth president**, was born in Kentucky.

Appositive phrases use commas the same way appositives do. If the phrase is not essential to a sentence, use commas. If it is essential, do not use commas.

My coworker **Mr. Schumacher** has visited Lincoln's birthplace.

- Do not confuse appositive phrases with **participial phrases.** A participial phrase is a participle and words that complete its meaning. It acts as an adjective.

Flipping through the pages, we found one of Lincoln's speeches.

Polar Bears

Is each underlined phrase an appositive phrase or a participial phrase?

20. The largest land carnivores, polar bears, live in the Arctic.
(A) appositive phrase (B) participial phrase

21. Weighing about 1,500 pounds, male polar bears are larger than females.
(A) appositive phrase (B) participial phrase

22. Strong swimmers, polar bears move up to four miles per hour underwater.
(A) appositive phrase (B) participial phrase

23. Consisting of hollow hairs, water-repellent fur lets them go long distances.
(A) appositive phrase (B) participial phrase

24. Black skin, another defense from the cold, absorbs heat under polar bear fur.
(A) appositive phrase (B) participial phrase

25. Their white fur, an additional protection, camouflages polar bears in snow.
(A) appositive phrase (B) participial phrase

Unit 14
Appositives

Uncle Sam

26. Uncle Sam, <u>a symbol of United States patriotism</u>, is thought to be named for a real person.
(A) appositive phrase **(B)** participial phrase

27. <u>Dressed in red, white, and blue</u>, he has been popular in political posters and cartoons since the first World War.
(A) appositive phrase **(B)** participial phrase

28. <u>Wearing a suit of his generation and a top hat</u>, Uncle Sam is easily recognized.
(A) appositive phrase **(B)** participial phrase

29. Samuel Wilson, <u>the man on which Uncle Sam is said to be based</u>, was born in 1766.
(A) appositive phrase **(B)** participial phrase

30. Ebenezer Wilson, <u>Samuel's brother</u>, relocated with him to Troy, New York, in 1789.
(A) appositive phrase **(B)** participial phrase

31. <u>A meatpacker during the War of 1812</u>, Samuel Wilson provided meat for the United States Army.
(A) appositive phrase **(B)** participial phrase

32. <u>Shipped carefully</u>, the meat was packed in barrels stamped with the initials "U.S."
(A) appositive phrase **(B)** participial phrase

33. The legend, <u>a tale now shared for over 100 years</u>, claims that someone thought the initials meant "Uncle Sam."
(A) appositive phrase **(B)** participial phrase

34. <u>Known for his appearance in the cartoons</u>, Samuel Wilson probably did not resemble the image we are familiar with today.
(A) appositive phrase **(B)** participial phrase

The Third LAP
Language Activity Pages

A. Exercising Your Skill

You have been learning about subjects, predicates, direct and indirect objects, appositives, appositive phrases, and participial phrases. Number your paper from 1 to 8. Read the sentences below. Use a word from the box only once to complete each sentence correctly.

complete	subject	appositive	direct
participial	predicate	indirect	sentence

1. A _____ has two main parts: a subject and a predicate.
2. A _____ subject or predicate includes the subject or predicate and any words that describe it or add to its meaning.
3. An _____ is next to the noun it gives more information about or modifies.
4. A _____ phrase acts as an adjective that includes a participle and other words to complete its meaning.
5. An object that is _____ answers the question *to what* or *to whom*.
6. An object that is _____ answers the question *what* or *whom*.
7. The _____ of a sentence tells whom or what a sentence is about.
8. The _____ tells what something is or what is being done in a sentence.

B. Expanding Your Skill

Number your paper from 1 to 8. Read the sentences below. Decide if each underlined phrase is an appositive phrase or a participial phrase. On your paper, write the letters **AP** for an appositive phrase or the letters **PP** for a participial phrase.

1. Harriet Tubman, <u>a very brave woman</u>, served as a scout for the Union Army during the Civil War.
2. <u>Gathering useful information</u>, she traveled through the South.
3. <u>Disguised as an old man</u>, Harriet passed on information about the plans of the Confederate Army.
4. Confederate troops, <u>enemies of the Union Army</u>, put a price on her head.
5. <u>Taking on important issues of her day</u>, Harriet helped to free slaves on the Underground Railroad.
6. This "railroad," <u>places where slaves safely hid during transport</u>, was not an actual railroad.
7. "Conductors," <u>people who worked the Underground Railroad</u>, risked a lot.
8. Harriet Tubman, <u>a helpful and generous woman</u>, will be remembered for her efforts.

C. Exploring Language

Narrative Writing Number your paper from 1 to 10. Read the brief biography below. Identify the underlined word or words by writing the letter **S** for subject, the letter **P** for predicate, the letters **DO** for direct object, or the letters **IO** for indirect object.

Harriet Tubman

(1) Harriet Tubman was born a slave, but she (2) lived and died a free person. She escaped a (3) plantation in the South and made her way to Pennsylvania by traveling at night. Harriet's journey (4) encouraged the creation of the Underground Railroad. Harriet built a decent (5) life for herself in the North. (6) She eventually worked as a nurse. Harriet completed several (7) trips back to the South and led more than 300 slaves to freedom. She (8) was proud to be a conductor on the Underground Railroad. Harriet never lost a "passenger" on any of her trips. Harriet Tubman gave many (9) people (10) hope.

D. Expressing Yourself

Choose one of these activities. When you are finished, give your paper to your teacher.

1. Think of a person you would choose for a biography. Draw a quick sketch of that person. Use an image of the person from a book, a magazine, or another reference source to look at while you draw him or her. Write the person's name above your drawing. Under your drawing, you will write four sentences. Write two sentences to describe the person and one sentence to tell about something he or she has accomplished. Write the last sentence to explain why you chose this person. Be sure to use one compound predicate, one direct object, and two appositive phrases in sentences of your choice.

2. WORK with a PARTNER Work with a partner to find a brief article in a newspaper or a magazine. Read carefully as you both search for any compound subjects, compound predicates, direct objects, and appositives in the article. On a separate sheet of paper, list and identify the words you found. Attach the article to your paper before turning it in.

Unit 15

Clauses

A **clause** is a group of words that has a subject and a predicate (verb). All sentences have at least one clause. There are two types of clauses.

- An **independent** or **main clause** can stand alone as a sentence.

  The train is late.

- A **dependent** or **subordinate clause** cannot stand alone. Even though a dependent clause has a subject and a predicate, it must be combined with an independent clause to form a sentence. A dependent clause can come before or after an independent clause. Many dependent clauses begin with a subordinating conjunction, such as *after, before, since, than, until*, and *while*.

  I will be glad **when the train arrives**. I wonder **if this happens often**.

  SUBORDINATING CONJUNCTION

The Statue of Liberty

Is the underlined clause in each sentence independent or dependent?

1. The Statue of Liberty was a gift from the people of France.
   (A) independent clause **(B)** dependent clause

2. While the French raised money for the statue, Americans collected funds for the base upon which it would stand.
   (A) independent clause **(B)** dependent clause

3. The statue took a long time to complete because it was so gigantic.
   (A) independent clause **(B)** dependent clause

4. Finally the statue was ready for its voyage to New York City.
   (A) independent clause **(B)** dependent clause

5. When it was taken apart to be shipped to America, sections of the statue filled 200 huge crates.
   (A) independent clause **(B)** dependent clause

6. After the crates were loaded onto a ship, the statue began its passage to America in May of 1885.
   (A) independent clause **(B)** dependent clause

Unit 15
Clauses

One way to join two or more independent clauses is to use a comma (,) with a coordinating conjunction. *And, but*, and *or* are coordinating conjunctions.

I left my lunch at home**, and** I did not have time to go back for it.

Another way to combine independent clauses is to use a semicolon (;). In this case, a coordinating conjunction is not used.

I owed my friend**;** he loaned me some money for lunch.

Bread

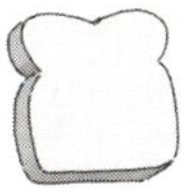

Is the underlined clause in each sentence independent or dependent?

7. Bread did not exist until Egyptians roasted grains of wheat over open fires.
(A) independent clause **(B)** dependent clause

8. When it was first made, bread did not taste the way it does today.
(A) independent clause **(B)** dependent clause

9. Bread of long ago was flatter because it had no yeast in it.
(A) independent clause **(B)** dependent clause

10. The Egyptians discovered yeast; the taste of bread improved.
(A) independent clause **(B)** dependent clause

11. After the dough was baked, it felt softer and lighter.
(A) independent clause **(B)** dependent clause

12. Bread was baked on flat stones, but Egyptians soon invented an oven.
(A) independent clause **(B)** dependent clause

13. Bread has an extended history; it has been nourishing people for a long time.
(A) independent clause **(B)** dependent clause

14. Today there are hundreds of varieties of bread.
(A) independent clause **(B)** dependent clause

Unit 15

Clauses

When a dependent clause comes before an independent clause in a sentence, the two clauses are separated by a comma.

While I waited for Hannah, I read some poetry.

↑ DEPENDENT CLAUSE ↑ INDEPENDENT CLAUSE

When a dependent clause comes after an independent clause that modifies the predicate in a sentence, a comma is not used.

We both went right home because we were tired.

↑ INDEPENDENT CLAUSE ↑ DEPENDENT CLAUSE

Atlanta

Are the underlined words in each sentence a dependent clause?

15. <u>If you have never been to Atlanta, Georgia</u>, it is a great place for a vacation.
   (A) Yes **(B)** No

16. <u>Atlanta was home to the 1996 Olympic Summer Games</u>.
   (A) Yes **(B)** No

17. Many of the Olympic buildings and beautiful grounds <u>are still there</u>.
   (A) Yes **(B)** No

18. You can visit the Martin Luther King Jr. National Historic Site <u>while you stay in Atlanta</u>.
   (A) Yes **(B)** No

19. <u>You could see Dr. King's birthplace</u>, or you could visit where he is buried.
   (A) Yes **(B)** No

20. <u>As the seasons change</u>, any time is a good time to vacation in Atlanta.
   (A) Yes **(B)** No

21. One of the very best times to go is in April <u>when trees and bushes bloom with red, pink, and white flowers</u>.
   (A) Yes **(B)** No

Unit 15
Clauses

Grizzly Bears 

Is the underlined clause in each sentence independent or dependent?

22. Pioneers hunted countless grizzly bears.
(A) independent clause **(B)** dependent clause

23. There were many more grizzly bears then than there are now.
(A) independent clause **(B)** dependent clause

24. Grizzlies are scarce; the habitat of the grizzly bear is disappearing.
(A) independent clause **(B)** dependent clause

25. Since the United States has very little wild country left without roads, these animals are limited to a few remaining patches of wilderness.
(A) independent clause **(B)** dependent clause

26. Approximately 1,200 grizzly bears still thrive in such wilderness areas of the United States.
(A) independent clause **(B)** dependent clause

27. Grizzly bears can be up to eight feet tall while they stand on their hind legs.
(A) independent clause **(B)** dependent clause

28. These bears can run very fast when they are chasing prey.
(A) independent clause **(B)** dependent clause

29. Grizzlies can put on a fat layer of nearly 400 pounds, but this typically occurs in the winter.
(A) independent clause **(B)** dependent clause

30. Grizzly bears eat a variety of food; they consume plants, berries, insects, fish, and other mammals.
(A) independent clause **(B)** dependent clause

Unit 15

Clauses

An **adjective clause** is a dependent clause that modifies, or describes, a noun or a pronoun in the main clause of a sentence. An adjective clause answers the question *what kind, how many*, or *which one*.

The route **that we took to the farm** was a detour.

An adjective clause usually begins with a **relative pronoun**, such as *that, which, who, whom*, or *whose*. A relative pronoun can often act as the subject in an adjective clause.

Ivy Road, **which is our usual route**, was closed.

Lewis and Clark

Are the underlined words in each sentence an adjective clause?

31. William Lewis and Meriwether Clark were soldiers and frontiersmen.
(A) Yes **(B)** No

32. Thomas Jefferson, who was the president of the United States in 1804, sent them into unclaimed territory on the western side of the Missouri River.
(A) Yes **(B)** No

33. Nothing could have prepared them for the hardships that they would face.
(A) Yes **(B)** No

34. In August of 1805, Lewis, Clark, and their group reached the Rocky Mountains, which became their greatest challenge.
(A) Yes **(B)** No

35. After crossing the mountains, they continued toward the Pacific Ocean.
(A) Yes **(B)** No

36. Many Native Americans, whom they met along the way, assisted them.
(A) Yes **(B)** No

37. Lewis and Clark, whose expedition had been a success, returned three years later upon claiming for the United States all the land between the Missouri River and the Pacific Ocean.
(A) Yes **(B)** No

Unit 15

Clauses

An **adverb clause** is a dependent clause that often modifies the verb in the main clause of a sentence. An adverb clause answers the question *when, where, why, how, to what degree*, or *under what conditions*.

If we win the game, we will celebrate.

An adverb clause begins with a subordinating conjunction.

This game is very important **because it is for the championship**.

- Do *not* confuse an adverb clause with a prepositional phrase. Some subordinating conjunctions and prepositions are the same. However, an adverb clause has a subject and a verb. A prepositional phrase has a noun or a pronoun.

We hung signs **before it rained**. We hung signs **before the game**.

The Art Museum

Is each underlined part an adverb clause or a prepositional phrase?

38. Before I visited the art museum, I was not very excited.
(A) adverb clause **(B)** prepositional phrase

39. I put off going until the last minute.
(A) adverb clause **(B)** prepositional phrase

40. I changed my mind after I got there.
(A) adverb clause **(B)** prepositional phrase

41. I did not know about the hands-on activities until I saw a program.
(A) adverb clause **(B)** prepositional phrase

42. I got to build a shadow-box collage before lunch.
(A) adverb clause **(B)** prepositional phrase

43. After I ate, I poured many different colors of sand into bottles.
(A) adverb clause **(B)** prepositional phrase

44. I took one more walk in the sculpture gallery before it was time to leave.
(A) adverb clause **(B)** prepositional phrase

45. As I left at the end of the day, I had a new attitude about art museums.
(A) adverb clause **(B)** prepositional phrase

Unit 16
Types of Sentences

A **simple sentence** contains one independent, or main, clause. The clause contains one subject and one predicate (verb).

The **fire caused** much damage to the forest.

A simple sentence's clause may have a compound subject or predicate.

Subject: Strong **winds** and dry **conditions** added to the damage.

Predicate: Firefighters **worked** steadily and finally **controlled** the fire.

A **compound sentence** contains two or more independent clauses. The clauses are joined by a comma (,) and a conjunction or by a semicolon (;).

The fire destroyed thousands of acres, **and** it was avoidable.

The cause was an abandoned campfire**;** this neglect had tragic results.

New Mexico

Is each sentence simple or compound?

1. New Mexico is a place of many different legends.
(A) simple sentence **(B)** compound sentence

2. An ancient civilization of Native Americans has left its mark on the land.
(A) simple sentence **(B)** compound sentence

3. The people disappeared long ago, but their amazing cliff homes remain.
(A) simple sentence **(B)** compound sentence

4. New Mexico was part of the "Wild West," and reminders are still there.
(A) simple sentence **(B)** compound sentence

5. Gunfighters and outlaws are also part of New Mexico's history.
(A) simple sentence **(B)** compound sentence

6. The first nuclear bomb was built in Los Alamos, and Roswell has been a tourist destination for years.
(A) simple sentence **(B)** compound sentence

7. Come to New Mexico; it is a beautiful and somewhat mysterious place.
(A) simple sentence **(B)** compound sentence

Unit 16
Types of Sentences

Arizona

8. We visited Arizona and had a terrific time.
(A) simple sentence **(B)** compound sentence

9. We saw some of the Grand Canyon; it was impressive.
(A) simple sentence **(B)** compound sentence

10. Some people may not think of snow in Arizona.
(A) simple sentence **(B)** compound sentence

11. There are places in northern Arizona with snow during certain times of the year.
(A) simple sentence **(B)** compound sentence

12. Phoenix, the capital of Arizona, is centrally located in the state.
(A) simple sentence **(B)** compound sentence

13. Phoenix has a zoo, museums, and numerous other things to do; Phoenix is also home to colleges and universities.
(A) simple sentence **(B)** compound sentence

14. The city of Tucson, a commonly mispronounced name, is located in the southern part of Arizona.
(A) simple sentence **(B)** compound sentence

15. Tucson was once part of Mexico, but it became a part of the United States in 1854.
(A) simple sentence **(B)** compound sentence

16. Both Phoenix and Tucson are an exciting mix of Mexican American, Native American, and American West cultures.
(A) simple sentence **(B)** compound sentence

17. Arizona has many delightful cities; we hope to visit Flagstaff or Yuma on our next vacation to Arizona.
(A) simple sentence **(B)** compound sentence

Unit 16
Types of Sentences

A **complex sentence** has one independent clause and one or more dependent clauses.

When we saw the site of the fire, | we could not believe the damage.

DEPENDENT CLAUSE — INDEPENDENT CLAUSE

It will be many years | before this forest recovers.

INDEPENDENT — DEPENDENT

Sacagawea

Is each sentence complex?

18. When Lewis and Clark started their expedition, they were not alone.
(A) Yes **(B)** No

19. Their crew of about forty-five men also included Sacagawea, a Native American woman.
(A) Yes **(B)** No

20. Sacagawea was the guide for the expedition; she arranged for the crew's safe passage through the Rockies.
(A) Yes **(B)** No

21. Sacagawea's brother and other Shoshone guides led the way through the Rockies, which was the most difficult part of the trip.
(A) Yes **(B)** No

22. Sacagawea's skill and knowledge, which were valued by Lewis and Clark, were critical to the success of the expedition.
(A) Yes **(B)** No

23. This amazing woman, who guided the expedition to the west coast and back, had the extra responsibility of traveling with her infant son.
(A) Yes **(B)** No

24. Lewis and Clark could not have completed their expedition without the help and bravery of others.
(A) Yes **(B)** No

Unit 16
Types of Sentences

Bats

Is each sentence simple, compound, or complex?

25. It is true that many people do not understand bats.
(A) simple sentence **(B)** compound sentence **(C)** complex sentence

26. That is too bad because bats are an important part of the ecosystem.
(A) simple sentence **(B)** compound sentence **(C)** complex sentence

27. The statement "All bats feed on blood" is incorrect.
(A) simple sentence **(B)** compound sentence **(C)** complex sentence

28. Many people would agree with that statement, but it is not true.
(A) simple sentence **(B)** compound sentence **(C)** complex sentence

29. Actually, only three known bat species feed on animal blood, and none of them live in the United States.
(A) simple sentence **(B)** compound sentence **(C)** complex sentence

30. The other bat species eat insects, nectar, and fruit.
(A) simple sentence **(B)** compound sentence **(C)** complex sentence

31. Bats, which are not blind, cannot see color.
(A) simple sentence **(B)** compound sentence **(C)** complex sentence

32. Some bats utilize *echolocation*, which helps them maneuver in darkness.
(A) simple sentence **(B)** compound sentence **(C)** complex sentence

33. *Echolocation* uses the echoes of certain animal sounds to detect obstacles or food in their paths.
(A) simple sentence **(B)** compound sentence **(C)** complex sentence

Unit 16

Types of Sentences

A **compound-complex sentence** has two or more independent clauses and at least one dependent clause.

[When the firefighters arrived,] [they worked fast,] and [soon the fire stopped.]

DEPENDENT CLAUSE — INDEPENDENT CLAUSES

More about Bats

Is each sentence compound-complex?

34. While there are many misconceptions about bats, they are very important to the ecosystem, and people need to know that.

(A) Yes **(B)** No

35. The millions and millions of insects that bats consume should make them our friends.

(A) Yes **(B)** No

36. One bat can eat nearly 600 insects an hour!

(A) Yes **(B)** No

37. I have read about many insects that are helpful to the environment, but I know too many would exist without bats.

(A) Yes **(B)** No

38. Bats that drink nectar pollinate many kinds of fruit throughout the world.

(A) Yes **(B)** No

39. Bats get pollen on their bodies as they move from flower to flower, and this helps spread the pollen over a wide area.

(A) Yes **(B)** No

40. Maybe people's attitudes will change as they understand more about bats, and bats will gain some of the respect that they have earned and deserve.

(A) Yes **(B)** No

Unit 16
Types of Sentences

Stalactites and Stalagmites

What is each type of sentence?

41. Stalactites and stalagmites form in different places.
(A) simple **(B)** compound **(C)** complex **(D)** compound-complex

42. Stalactites and stalagmites may look like cones without ice cream, but they are both minerals left over from water that evaporates in caves.
(A) simple **(B)** compound **(C)** complex **(D)** compound-complex

43. A cave has to have limestone before stalactites and stalagmites can form.
(A) simple **(B)** compound **(C)** complex **(D)** compound-complex

44. Groundwater that is above the cave seeps through the roof of the cave.
(A) simple **(B)** compound **(C)** complex **(D)** compound-complex

45. This water dissolves the limestone as it drips onto the cave's floor.
(A) simple **(B)** compound **(C)** complex **(D)** compound-complex

46. When the water evaporates, there are minerals left behind, and over many years the mineral layers build up.
(A) simple **(B)** compound **(C)** complex **(D)** compound-complex

47. Stalactites hang from the ceiling of a cave; stalagmites form on the floor of a cave.
(A) simple **(B)** compound **(C)** complex **(D)** compound-complex

48. Stalagmites appear to grow upward, and they look like upside-down cones.
(A) simple **(B)** compound **(C)** complex **(D)** compound-complex

49. I wonder if the tips of a stalactite and a stalagmite could touch and become one.
(A) simple **(B)** compound **(C)** complex **(D)** compound-complex

50. If the tips did touch, I think the weaker tip would crumble, but the stronger tip would remain intact.
(A) simple **(B)** compound **(C)** complex **(D)** compound-complex

The Last LAP

Language Activity Pages

A. Exercising Your Skill

You have been learning about independent, dependent, adjective, and adverb clauses. Building on such skills, you have learned about simple, compound, complex, and compound-complex sentences. Number your paper from 1 to 8. Read the sentences below. Use a word from the box only once to complete each sentence correctly.

compound	adjective	complex	Independent
adverb	simple	Dependent	compound-complex

1. An _____ clause modifies a noun or a pronoun in the main clause of a sentence.
2. An _____ clause often modifies a verb in the main clause of a sentence.
3. _____, or subordinate, clauses cannot stand alone.
4. _____, or main, clauses can stand alone.
5. A _____ sentence has two or more independent clauses and at least one dependent clause.
6. A _____ sentence has one independent clause.
7. A _____ sentence has one independent clause and at least one dependent clause.
8. A _____ sentence has two or more independent clauses.

B. Expanding Your Skill

Number your paper from 1 to 6. Read the book review below. Look carefully at each group of underlined words. If the underlined words are an independent clause, write the letter **I** on your paper. If the words are a dependent clause, then write the letter **D** on your paper.

Sarah, Plain and Tall

The author of this book is Patricia MacLachlan. **(1)** <u>It is the story of a pioneer family.</u> **(2)** <u>When the family's mother passes away,</u> the father realizes that he cannot care for them and do all the work on the farm. He wants someone to come and take care of his children. **(3)** <u>After he puts an advertisement in the newspaper,</u> **(4)** <u>a girl named Sarah answers it.</u> She cares for the children, and eventually, they become a family of their own. **(5)** <u>I liked this book</u> **(6)** <u>because it gave a lot of information about pioneer life.</u>

C. Exploring Language

Expository Writing Number your paper from 1 to 6. Read the book review below. Look carefully at each underlined sentence. If the underlined sentence is a simple sentence, write the letter **S** on your paper. If the underlined sentence is a compound sentence, write the letters **CP** on your paper. For a complex sentence, write the letters **CX** on your paper. Finally, if the underlined sentence is a compound-complex sentence, write the letters **CPCX** on your paper.

Mrs. Frisby and the Rats of NIMH

(1) <u>This book was written by Robert C. O'Brien.</u> It is the story of a group of superior rats that escape from a laboratory. (2) <u>They are aware of the mistakes that human beings have made, and they want to avoid making the same ones.</u> (3) <u>At first they live close to humans.</u> The rats use some equipment to get the food, electricity, and water that they need from human society. (4) <u>Since stealing is wrong, the rats decide to come up with a different plan.</u> (5) <u>They eventually move away to an isolated place; there the rats begin to develop a civilization of their own.</u> (6) <u>I like this book because the story was unusual.</u> Also, it was interesting trying to understand things from an animal's point of view.

D. Expressing Yourself

Choose one of these activities. When you are finished, give your work to your teacher.

1. Make a bookmark that goes with the topic of a story you have read recently. Draw a design or a picture on the bookmark that matches or goes with the story. On the back of the bookmark, write at least one simple and one compound sentence. Use the sentences to tell something about the story and to tell why you like the story. You should have at least two sentences.
2. WORK with a PARTNER Find a partner, and choose a book from your classroom together. Flip to a page of the book that has at least one paragraph on it. If there are many paragraphs on the page, then select just one of them. Work with your partner to identify any adjective clauses or adverb clauses that are used. If there is time left or neither type of clause was used, look for compound sentences in the paragraph. Write what you both find on one sheet of paper.

GRAMMAR Scope and Sequence • *Specific Skill Series for Language Arts*

Unit/Level	Level A	Level B	Level C	Level D	Level E	Level F	Level G	Level H
Unit 1	Nouns	Nouns	Nouns	Nouns	Nouns	Nouns	Nouns	Nouns
Unit 2	Singular and Plural Nouns	Singular and Plural Nouns	Singular and Plural Nouns	Possessive Nouns	Possessive Nouns	Possessive Nouns	Possessive Nouns	Possessive Nouns
Unit 3	Possessive Nouns	Possessive Nouns	Possessive Nouns	Subject and Object Pronouns	Subject and Object Pronouns	Subject and Object Pronouns	Subject and Object Pronouns	Subject and Object Pronouns
Unit 4	Pronouns	Pronouns	Pronouns	Possessive Pronouns	Possessive Pronouns	Possessive Pronouns	Possessive Pronouns	Possessive Pronouns
Unit 5	Possessive Pronouns	Possessive Pronouns	Subject and Object Pronouns	Pronouns	Pronouns	Pronouns	Pronouns	Pronouns
Unit 6	Verbs	Interrogative Pronouns	Possessive Pronouns	Pronouns	Pronouns	Pronouns	Pronouns	Pronouns
Unit 7	Helping Verbs	Verbs	Interrogative Pronouns	Verbs	Verbs	Verbs	Verbs	Verbs
Unit 8	Adjectives	Helping Verbs	Verbs	Adjectives	Adjectives	Adjectives	Adjectives	Adjectives
Unit 9	Parts of a Sentence	Adjectives	Helping Verbs	Adverbs	Adverbs	Adverbs	Adverbs	Adverbs
Unit 10	Parts of a Sentence	Adverbs	Adjectives	Prepositions	Prepositions	Prepositions	Prepositions	Prepositions
Unit 11	Changing Sentences into Questions	Prepositions	Adverbs	Interjections and Conjunctions	Conjunctions	Conjunctions	Conjunctions	Conjunctions
Unit 12	Changing Sentences into Questions	Conjunctions	Prepositions	Subjects and Predicates	Subjects and Predicates	Subjects and Predicates	Subjects and Predicates	Subjects and Predicates
Unit 13		Interjections	Conjunctions	Direct Objects	Direct and Indirect Objects	Direct and Indirect Objects	Direct and Indirect Objects	Direct and Indirect Objects
Unit 14		Parts of a Sentence	Interjections	Clauses	Appositives	Appositives	Appositives	Appositives
Unit 15		Compound Subjects and Predicates	Subjects and Predicates	Clauses	Clauses	Gerunds	Gerunds	Gerunds
Unit 16		Changing Sentences into Questions	Compound Subjects and Predicates	Types of Sentences	Types of Sentences	Clauses	Infinitives	Infinitives
Unit 17		Changing Sentences into Questions	Complete Subjects and Predicates			Types of Sentences	Clauses	Clauses
Unit 18			Types of Sentences				Types of Sentences	Clauses
Unit 19			Changing Sentences into Questions					Types of Sentences